SHIGA THE POTTER

For Nicola and Julian

SHIGA THE POTTER

Photographs JUTTA MALNIC
Interviews with Shiga BOB THOMPSON

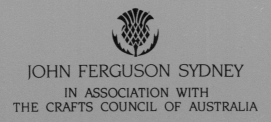

JOHN FERGUSON SYDNEY

IN ASSOCIATION WITH
THE CRAFTS COUNCIL OF AUSTRALIA

First published in 1982 by
John Ferguson Pty Ltd
133 Macquarie Street
Sydney NSW 2000

The publisher gratefully acknowledges
the assistance given to this book
by the Japan Foundation.

National Library of Australia
Cataloguing-in-publication data.

Shiga.

Shiga the potter.

ISBN 0 909134 53 7.

1. Shiga. 2. Pottery, Japanese.
I. Malnic, Jutta. II. Thompson, Bob.
III. Title.

738′.092′4

Designed by Judy Hungerford
Typeset by Savage & Co Pty Ltd, Queensland.
Printed in Singapore by Kyodo Printing.

CONTENTS

INTRODUCTION

How did we first meet Shiga-san? In this case, the old saying that 'great events cast their shadows ahead' seems particularly apt: I knew Shiga's pots and I wanted to know the man who made them.

Thus one Sunday in 1976 our mutual friends Yayoi and Paul Maloney arranged for my husband and me to meet Shiga at his Terrey Hills pottery on the outskirts of Sydney.

There we met Elaine and Bob Thompson and on that wintry day we all sat in the sunny opening of Shiga's chicken shed turned pottery — talking, drinking coffee out of bumped-about mugs and enjoying our instant friendship.

Inside the shed, gleaming in reflected sunlight, were shelves laden with ceramics. We saw some very large bowls and I wondered how a man so short of stature could have managed to throw them. I picked up a round lidded jar with oilspot glaze and felt that meeting that jar was like meeting a person.

Deeper in the darkness of the shed, waiting to be placed in the kiln, were shadow armies of biscuitted and drying pots as well as stacks of loose brick, clay and glaze material in basins, bowls, buckets and bags. Next to and on the window benches were potter's wheels and a stool, as well as jars with wire, brushes, sticks, knives and spatulas. In short, the mess of creativity.

Shiga spoke to us about the difficulties of achieving a perfect oilspot glaze and the degree of accuracy required in mixing, glazing and firing. I seem to remember that he said this glaze was 'like the dark Milky Way of our dreams', which I liked very much.

To reinforce what he had been saying about the problems associated with this glaze, Shiga showed us several boxes of imperfectly glazed pots in the back paddock, work he dismissed as 'throw-outs' and 'rubbish'. Very reluctantly he allowed me to scavenge two bowls; I have used them in my kitchen every single day since then.

Some time later, the Maloneys brought Shiga-san to visit us. After that, he came to our home several times. He always spent some time quietly by himself, wandering around the house and the garden. He said he loved our house.

Once, when he brought us a present, I unwrapped it too quickly and broke the lid of a sugar bowl. We did not mention this terrible incident again but later, when I was handling and photographing his own precious collection, Shiga must have been stiff with worry.

Time flew past and Shiga was ready to return to Japan. He was all packed; his final exhibitions had been sold out. You could say that Australia farewelled him like a very personal friend. On the opening night of his retrospective exhibition in August 1979, many of us already felt in a state of loss as we listened to his speech. Surrounding us, his audience, was the display of an astounding and exquisite selection of his pottery, each piece a representative sample kept from firings made during Shiga's thirteen years in Australia.

Suddenly the idea for this book appeared in my head and, like a searchlight, it illuminated the steps I must take to realise such a project. It seemed to me that the book could reflect to all Australians, whether descendants of early settlers or recent immigrants, the impact of this continent that all newcomers have felt in their own way. I decided to photograph the pots so that they would speak to us of Shiga's years in Australia, invoking a unique situation: a Japanese man who was one of us, a friend, who lived, loved and expressed himself in his art, who had been inspired by the essence of this country — bush, sky, soil and intensity of colour — and by the jubilant largesse of everything, and who had given expression and form, texture and colour to it.

I knew I would photograph Shiga's pots against the background of the bush, the gum trees and bark that gave him ash glazes.

Sometimes during his stay in Australia, Shiga had longed for the disciplines of Japan: for Buddhism, traditional conversations with his peers, rooms with *tatami* and *shoji* and the *tokonoma*. Then his pots had shown a realignment with Japanese thought forms, motifs and decorations and the imponderable digressions of *mingei*. I thought of setting these pots in soft light

and placing them on suitably coloured and textured hand-made papers.

These thoughts had their own impetus. Everyone I asked rushed to co-operate with the execution of the book. Shiga was definitely leaving for Japan; I was leaving for an extended stay in Papua New Guinea. Everything had to happen fast; the photographs were taken in a few days with excellent camera assistance from Nicola Malnic.

Bob Thompson who had also admired Shiga for some years, interviewed him for the book, and these interviews brought forth new and deep dimensions of Shiga's personality. Shiga spoke in Japanese, as it was felt important that he should be quoted correctly, and Christine Lawrence translated so fluently that we, crammed into my dark room, viewing the pots transparency by transparency, were often unaware that a language barrier was being crossed until Shiga himself shifted to English, modifying or confirming our grasp of his philosophy.

In this book we have tried to show Shiga's experience in Australia through his work and his words. He left us with the image of a great, mature man and artist.

Thank you, Shiga-san.

Thirty-one years ago, I started to work on pottery and of these thirty-one years I have spent thirteen in this country. My study of the art of pottery started on the basis of my study of the art of tea, calligraphy and Zen Buddhism.

In Kyoto, the ancient capital of Japan, I went to an art institute and there, under a certain master, I started my apprenticeship, in which I matured not only technically but spiritually. The major point I studied under the master was the technique of glazing, but since those early days I have been studying the whole art of pottery. Today I am aware of a sense of maturity with which, by simply looking at the work of other potters, I can tell what that potter's life philosophy may be, his or her level of expertise and artistry, perhaps something about his or her own lifestyle, even his or her physical characteristics.

When I studied in Kyoto I used to know an old artist. To my great surprise, in his workshop he simply used mechanical measures in mixing glazes. I was astounded that this old master was able to use his intuition in effecting an optimal mixture of different types of glazes and that, furthermore, the end product of that intuitive approach was so awesome. Nowadays, perhaps because I am ageing or perhaps because I have accomplished some satisfactory level of artistry, I am now able to understand that old master's intuition.

The Japanese way of learning, especially in an artistic sense, focuses on the importance of patience. By experiencing the long and sound practice of patience, which could be full of agony and, at times, perhaps ecstasy, I feel that it is through that sort of process that one can attain a certain sort of truth. I believe that this particular way of attaining truth is not unique to the Japanese alone; I am aware that the same truth applies to a large number of accomplished artists throughout the world.

Now, more specifically, when I come to regard what is really my art, especially in the formal sense, my most fundamental premise is simplicity. You probably realise that, among some of the work I have created during my stay in Australia are some pieces of work that are completely white in colour. When I was creating various pieces using no other colour but white, I was actually going through a very sad part of my life, during which some of my close relatives died. Those sad days made me search even more deeply for the meaning of human life, and it was with that searching that the colour white emerged. That was my expression of the state of life I was experiencing at the time.

Since I came to this country, I have had many opportunities to reflect about what Australia is and what or who Australians are; furthermore, being in a somewhat objective environment, I have had many opportunities to reflect on what Japan is. I am sure that you would appreciate, by looking at the work I have created so far, that I have absorbed a certain feeling about this country. I cannot exactly pinpoint what parts of this land influenced my work, but the blue sky and blue water of Sydney have certainly given me some impetus which, in turn, has been reflected in my art. These are not the only significant things; there are many, many countless things that have given impact to and influenced my art.

I am going back to Japan, where no doubt I will continue my life philosophy and lifestyle as I have done over the past thirteen years or so, primarily seeking truth, goodness and beauty. I will certainly cherish most profoundly the friendship you have extended to me.

It is inevitable that, in different parts of the world, potters should produce different kinds of art because they are influenced by the environment and the weather.

But there are other influences that account for the differences in pottery between one country and another.

In Japan, people have a strong affinity with nature that is reflected in the artistic tradition, whereas in the West, the philosophic tradition emphasises the self.

This means that the self always appears in the work of Western potters, no matter where they work.

I do not believe that the objective is to express one's self, but to bring out what is best in the clay.

The aim is not to learn technique, but to transcend technique, and the effort is not so much to improve your work, as your total self. This is why in Japan so many people practise arts such as brush painting or archery: they are means of self-development.

It is important to realise that this development is a continuous process in which nothing lasts; each act and each moment is important in itself.

The moment has gone; the development goes on.

Shigeo Shiga

SHIGA THE POTTER

Ash is a simple glaze; not a primitive glaze, but simple, preceding technology, and capable of producing subtle effects, pleasing in their simplicity. I spent time discovering the materials available to me and, before experimenting with other glazes, I tested some wood ash.
The smaller pot has a hardwood ash glaze from a local gum tree. The other has a softwood ash glaze from a pine tree such as I made in Japan. This softwood ash gave me a benchmark against which to judge the unfamiliar hard wood.

One of the first glazes with which I experimented
was a combination of pink and purple.
I had seen an unusual patch of purple-coloured
road dirt out in the countryside, and I was
fascinated by the wide variety of pink colours
in and around the gardens where I was working.
It was a particular pink creeper that first
made me realise how different Australia is
from Japan. In Japan we have lots of pink
flowers, but here was a creeper with pink
leaves, and so many different pinks.

There are no special associations, however,
to the purple glaze.
Rather it is a glaze that I experimented with
over many years, applying it to a range of
practical or familiar forms.
Speaking generally, I believe in the discipline
that a strong mastery of technical detail gives
the potter. It is no use having good ideas if you
cannot execute them. This is why I have always
studied materials and glazes, applying them
in a variety of ways.

It was when I moved away from the countryside,
oddly enough, that I began to question and
discover for myself what was unique to Australia.
In the countryside, I had lived in a timbered
home. Suddenly in Sydney, the homes were all
made of brick. Their dry texture led me to
experiment with these unglazed pieces,
decorated simply with 'chattering'.
In Japan, this technique of 'chattering' is used
very lightly and subtly to make 'footsteps'
(*tobigana*). Here I transformed the whole
surface of the pot, decorating the dry finished
surface with patterns of incisions.

Sydney was Australia: the blue sky and the sea
and the red tiled roofs of the houses. Those
were unique and they made me realise that I
must produce uniquely Australian work.
This crystalline blue mirrors the spiritual impact
that those first impressions of Sydney made on me.
Looking out over the beach, everything
is blue. It is almost too bright: the sun, the sea
and the sky are intense.

I began combining the purple glaze with pink,
and went on doing so right through my years
in Australia. Pots such as this one
were my most successful
achievements with these colours.

I made a series of pots which, I felt, particularly
expressed a new-found freedom in my potting.
Some Japanese friends, to whom I showed pots
such as this, were repelled. They said they had
a 'meaty' or 'oily' quality that they could not
accept. They were not Eastern.
From their reaction, I knew I had succeeded
in my objective.

In contrast with that freedom, I feel the broad
base of this urn establishes a feeling of peace,
the stability acquired through Zazen meditation.
The idea for such a lidded pot, with a handle
like the flame finial on the Buddha's head, came
to me during meditation, at a time when I found
renewed interest in Buddhist teachings as
compared with Western philosophy.
But it was not until much later that I understood
how this Buddhist self-searching process had
consistently influenced my work.

Only a few months before I left Australia,
I realised that, no matter what changes had
occurred during my stay, each year I had made
something with *tenmoku* glazing.
It was not until I reviewed the various ways in
which I had used it that I really understood the
creative forces inside me.
I realised that the use of the black *tenmoku* glaze
denoted the Buddhist self-searching process
within me, and that my whole inner being was
strongly Japanese. While the conscious
searchings I made led me to produce certain
pieces that others liked, and one must
be considerate of others, it was the
continuing, unconscious use of *tenmoku* glaze
that projected my underlying self.

In my personal aesthetic, my universe, the circle
is very important. I find it significant that animals
do not recognise circles; humans do. I like the
round shape of my pots, and there are times,
too, when I just like things to be 'pretty'. The
round shape of this pot, combined with the blue
and rose glaze, gives me that feeling.
While no particular symbolism is attached to it,
I did notice that many women chose to buy
such pots for an older person; perhaps
a parent or a sick friend.
I thought this was important, for, while a work
should give the artist personal satisfaction, it is
important that it should have a healing quality,
bringing peace, relief from pain,
or happiness to others.

There were times, certainly, when I wanted a very 'rough' pot, but not always. In fact, sometimes quite the opposite.
Here I wanted very fine pottery, with a very delicate, light celadon glaze applied over 'chattering' and displaying the Zen symbol of three dots, signifying beauty and truth.

This shape comes from China. It is the shape of the traditional medicine box. The Buddha of Healing, Yakushinyorai, is always shown holding such a bowl.
The *yuteki* (oil spot) glaze on the bowl to the right is an extremely difficult technical achievement, one with which I struggled at this time. It has mystical associations for me, expressing the feeling that one has sometimes while searching the black night sky and seeing, in the background to the stars, a fainter light.

When I settled into my workshop on the
outskirts of Sydney in 1972, I felt established.
1972 and 1974-75 were fruitful years for me.
I had many ideas stored up and I knew
what materials were available.
I had more energy than I have now. I had very
strong feelings and expressed them in these
strong, simple forms, slightly off-centre.
The glazes are also very simple, although they
were thickly applied, forming very strong ridges.

I was developing some of the very important
principles underlying the appreciation of beauty
that is a very important aspect of the tea
ceremony. In that cult, symmetry in shape and
honesty in materials are very important factors.
A machine-made shape with symmetry
imposed on it is unacceptable.
Here the spontaneity is signalled by the
unglazed area left by my fingerprint,
and the simplicity by the glaze.

The same honesty or simplicity in materials,
form, and decoration can show itself
in more severe taste.
But while the details differ, the subtlety — the
important quality — is constant, gentle.

It is the dryness echoed in this vase that is unique to Australia, while the patterns have many meanings: the waves on the ocean, the abstract, raked patterns in the garden of the Ryoanji Temple in Kyoto and the immense parallel sand ridges that dominate the deserts.

The sheer size of this pot and in particular the colour recalled what I saw in the red centre of Australia in 1972, when I went into the Simpson Desert with a Japanese friend.

I had a feeling that this *Shino* glaze could suit
Australia, echoing the dryness and the colours
I found in its landscape.

Similarly, the metallic red in this dish, harsher
and harder than the colours of Japan, signifies
the style and energy of a different land.
Before I came to Australia I knew how to
produce the glaze for this particular pot, but
I had never called on the knowledge.

Even with simple forms or apparently mundane objects such as this dish, there can be a creative skill in the repetitive acts of turning the pot and of dipping and distributing glazes. There is freedom in the unpremeditated routine of the potter and a certain mystery in the results it produces.

I think it is very important to stress that potting
is not an industrial technique, nor is it
simply a skill.
One does not plan a pot, not with the rational
mind. One makes the pot, building it through
the way in which the hands and
feelings run together.
As I made this, which I find a particularly Eastern
vase, I imagined the flowers already in it.

During the period of profound depression
I experienced after my younger brother
died, I used two glazes, the white and the
tenmoku, in his memory.
But the shape of this pot is a particular
memorial to him. The fuller shape reflects his
generosity of spirit: he was always more
concerned with other people than himself and he
was especially close to me. This is my brother.

I was working, preoccupied, and deeply shocked
by the death of my younger brother and I found
this shape evolving in a completely unexpected
way. The pot was almost completed when I
simply held my hands at the top and pushed
down, reaching for a point in the universe,
without thinking at all.
So, you see, design transcends thought, evolving
from the hands and the heart together.
This is essence, purity, nothing added . . .

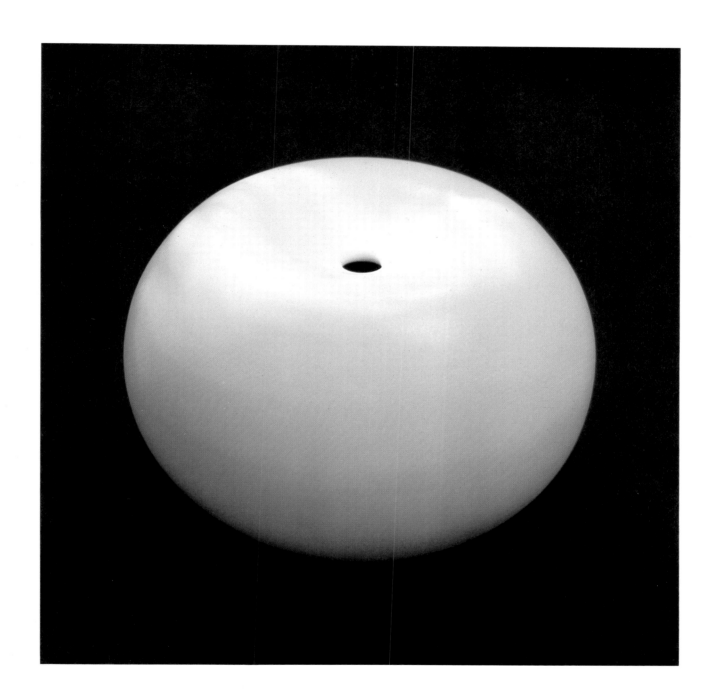

In the Eastern world, celadon has
a mystical significance.
When I knew that I would be leaving Australia,
I began mentally to move away. In a conscious
reappraisal, I stopped making large, colourful
pieces and worked towards unmeasured and
spontaneous glazes such as this soft green
celadon with 'chattering' under the glaze.

In the snow country of Japan, the ideograph
(*kanji*) decorating this pot signifies good tidings
— Spring is coming; happy days are here. The
three dots are from the Zen philosophy,
signifying truth — virtue, goodness, beauty.
I would say that, while the form and the colour
of this pot are Korean, it expressed my growing
feeling that I should return to Japan.

Blue and white brushwork is a very traditional
form of artistic expression and mastering control
of the brush to give light and perspective to a
setting is very difficult technically. Working in this
way, I reasserted what had been taught me first.
I was satisfying myself that I could work
this way in Japan.
This is an imaginary landscape, not an Australian
landscape but one created in my mind.
I saw the moon and I anticipated Japan; I saw
a peaceful landscape, quiet in my mind.

This is from the second last firing I made before
I returned to Japan. In future I shall concentrate
on simple glazes such as this, with some three
or four ingredients mixed by instinct, without
measuring, to give a very natural feeling
to the pot.
In this way I can express what I see as
truly Japanese elements.

I was born in Tokyo on 29 October 1928. When I was four years old, my parents decided to return to their family home in Takada, Niigata Prefecture. Niigata is on the north-western coast of the island of Honshu and the four seasons are very distinct there. I specially remember the beautiful pure white landscapes after the snow, and the patterns of the trees.

My father ran his own business, quite a large *sake* shop, and I had three brothers and three sisters. As I was the oldest son, I had a very traditional upbringing, because I was expected to take over the business later. Even when I was a child, I was responsible for helping my father take care of my brothers, sisters and younger cousins, and they were taught to show me respect.

Unfortunately, I was rather a weak child, small for my age and poor at sports. Until I was ten I spent most of my time inside — reading a lot, painting, doing craft work and practising music.

My father came from an old family, with a long history, and his brothers and uncles lived nearby. They were well educated and particularly interested in calligraphy, Oriental history and Confucian philosophy. Since I spent a lot of time inside with them, they had a strong influence on me.

When I was eleven, I went to the country to stay on my grandparents' farm for a few months. My grandmother knew a lot about natural herbal medicine and treated me during this time. I grew much stronger and became more interested in sport, but I remained the smallest in my family.

I went to the local school until I finished junior high school and during this time my father insisted that I should have extra coaching after school because I was the eldest. Then he sent me to a high school that specialised in bookkeeping and commercial studies to prepare me to take over the shop. In fact, I was not interested in business; I was much more interested in history. It was at this time that I began to study English — two hours a week of English was compulsory for all high school students until the end of 1944. However, I did not learn to speak English until I came to Australia.

When I finished high school I went to university, but dropped out after two years. This was just after the war, and it seemed to us all then that Japan had no future, and nor did we. My friend's father, an educated man, told me that it was particularly important to practise self-control in this situation, and suggested that I study some traditional art to help me do so. Many artists and teachers had moved from Tokyo to the country at this time, so I began to study the tea ceremony with a very good teacher who had come to live nearby. She noticed how much I appreciated the beautiful pots we used, and suggested that I study pottery.

My first teacher, Saburo Saito, had come back from the war in Manchuria with nothing. He had no workshop. His brother was a Zen monk in Niigata and he allowed us to build a workshop in the temple. I lived at the temple with the boys who were studying to become monks, and prayed and worked with them as well as studying pottery. It was very good training for me.

My father's business had failed during the war, and he had gone to work for another company. He was disappointed that I had decided to study pottery rather than go into business. It was hard to find a job at that time, and I actually rejected the offer of a job in a local bank. My apprenticeship was a long one — ten years — and

if I had been working and earning money, it would have been a great help to my family.

In Kyoto, one of my teachers was Kunio Uchida, who later, in 1959, introduced me to John Chappell, a young English potter who had just come to study with him. I helped John to set up his own workshop after he left Uchida, and we became good friends. It was John who introduced me to Les Blakesborough and his wife Sue when he came to study in Japan in 1963.

Three years later I went to Australia, planning to stay only about three or four years. I stayed at Sturt outside Mittagong on the southern tablelands of New South Wales from July 1966 to April 1968, and then worked with Bernie Sahm until December 1971.

I met my wife Alexandra very soon after I arrived in Mittagong; she was studying at Sturt. We married in April 1968.

I held my first exhibition in Australia in 1967 at Von Bertouch's Gallery in Newcastle, and had a major one-man show every eighteen months to two years after that. I had several exhibitions in Sydney, Melbourne, Canberra, Brisbane and Newcastle, and one each in Armidale, Adelaide and Fremantle.

In 1971, my father contracted stomach cancer and I returned to Japan in January of the following year. My father died a month later, and I stayed until May to arrange his funeral and organise his affairs, after which I came back to Australia.

I decided to set up my own workshop in a rural area in 1972 because of the council restrictions on pottery kilns in residential areas. The closest places to Sydney that were still zoned as rural then were Dural and Terrey Hills and for about three months we looked at every piece of land for sale in those areas. One of the reasons why I chose Terrey Hills was that several brick companies had clay pits nearby, so good local clay was available. I worked in a chicken shed surrounded by natural bush, feeling that I could experience the size of the country there and make big pots to suit such a big country. It was very different from the typical Japanese workshop, which is usually very small.

I returned to Japan again in 1975 when my younger brother was ill. It was a very sad time for me.

In February 1976, I was knocked down by a hit-and-run driver outside a hall in suburban Sydney. My left leg was broken just below the knee, and it was about four months before I started work again. Even then, the muscles were wasted, so I had a great deal of trouble throwing pots, as I have always sat at the wheel in the Japanese way, with my legs crossed. After the accident I was unable to hold that position for more than ten or fifteen minutes at a time. This meant that I had to make smaller pots, as the very large round pots and platters I had been making before the accident took one or two hours to make.

I left Australia in 1979, and have been working in Japan ever since. I have built my own workshop and kiln here on the outskirts of Tokyo; the workshop is about the size of a four-car garage, with a 70 cubic foot LP gas kiln. It is surrounded by chestnut trees with vegetable gardens and paddy fields nearby, so it also has an open feeling, but it is very different from Australia.

Shigeo Shiga

CATALOGUE

Pots, incised decoration, ash glazes
1967
Sturt, New South Wales
Left: height 13.75 cm
diameter 12.75 cm
Right: height 15.25 cm
diameter 13 cm

Jar, cut sides, white glaze with mauve
    splashes
1969
Sturt, New South Wales
height 13.5 cm diameter 13.5 cm

Plate, pale blue glaze with mauve
    splashes
1976
Terrey Hills, New South Wales
height 10 cm diameter 48 cm

Round pot, unglazed, chattered
    decoration
1970
Balmoral, New South Wales
height 21.8 cm diameter 23 cm

Pot, turquoise crystal glaze
1968
Balmoral, New South Wales
height 21.5 cm diameter 20.5 cm

Vase, pink and purple glaze
1972
Terrey Hills, New South Wales
height 22.3 cm diameter 13.3 cm

Vase, white glaze, slip decoration
1974
Terrey Hills, New South Wales
height 24 cm diameter 23 cm

Lidded urn, *tenmoku* and iron glazes
1975
Terrey Hills, New South Wales
height 22 cm diameter 23 cm

Hexagonal urn, *tenmoku* glaze
1978
Terrey Hills, New South Wales
height 20.75 cm diameter 19.5 cm

Round pot, blue and rose glaze
1975
Terrey Hills, New South Wales
height 18 cm diameter 18.25 cm

Bowl, chattered decoration, celadon
  glaze, three red dots
1978
Terrey Hills, New South Wales
height 7.5 cm diameter 22.5 cm

Medicine boxes
1973
Terrey Hills, New South Wales
Left: White glaze
height 8.75 cm diameter 9.75 cm
Right: Oilspot *tenmoku* glaze
height 7.5 cm diameter 9.5 cm

Jar, *Shino*-type glaze
1972
Terrey Hills, New South Wales
height 24 cm diameter 18.5 cm

Tea cup, ash glaze
1974
Terrey Hills, New South Wales
height 7.2 cm diameter 5.5 cm

Lidded pot, *tenmoku* glaze, iron glaze
decoration
1967
Sturt, New South Wales
height 8.5 cm diameter 11.5 cm

Slab pot, wire cut sides
1972
Terrey Hills, New South Wales
height 32.25 cm diameter 12.5 cm

Very large floor pot, incised
decoration, *Shino*-type glaze
1975
Terrey Hills, New South Wales
height 42 cm diameter 41 cm

Square plate, incised decoration,
Shino-type glaze
1972
Terrey Hills, New South Wales
height 6.5 cm 28.5 cm square

Large bowl, tomato glaze, iron and
 white glaze decoration with red
 dots
1976
Terrey Hills, New South Wales
height 10 cm diameter 48 cm

Bowl, pink and purple glaze
1968
Sturt, New South Wales
height 55 cm diameter 18 cm

Vase, black and white glazes
1978
Terrey Hills, New South Wales
height 25 cm diameter 16 cm

Round pot, *tenmoku* glaze, iron glaze
 decoration
1974
Terrey Hills, New South Wales
height 20 cm diameter 21 cm

Round pot, white glaze
1975
Terrey Hills, New South Wales
height 20.5 cm diameter 26.5 cm

Bottle, chattered decoration,
 celadon glaze
1978
Terrey Hills, New South Wales
height 20 cm diameter 16.5 cm

Plate, *tenmoku* glaze, iron glaze
    decoration with three red dots
1978
Terrey Hills, New South Wales
height 5.5 cm diameter 32.5 cm

Small bottle, landscape drawn with
    cobalt
1979
Terrey Hills, New South Wales
height 15.5 cm diameter 10.75 cm

Round pot, greyish mottled glaze,
    brushed decoration with red dots
1979
Terrey Hills, New South Wales
height 21.5 cm diameter 20.5 cm